THE STRATEGIC PLAN GUIDE

From the

FAST-TRACK BUSINESS EXPERT SERIES ™ OF BOOKS AND COURSES

Mark A. Philip
2012

THE STRATEGIC PLAN GUIDE

From the
FAST-TRACK BUSINESS EXPERT SERIES ™ OF BOOKS AND COURSES

BY MARK A. PHILIP

A Management Guide To Developing A Strategic Planning Process

The Strategic Plan Guide provides a step-by-step management guide of a strategic planning process, which will result in the development of a well-thought through, comprehensive strategic plan for your business.

Copyright © 2012 Mark Philip

THE STRATEGIC PLAN GUIDE

Companies without a strategic plan can meander from one new tactic to the next, lack focus and a clear message, confuse customers, and create underperforming products. A strategy does not need to be complex, and does not need to take long to prepare, but it does need some thought and good understanding of your potential customers and the marketplace.

I am excited to provide you with a strategic planning process for your growing business, whether small or large. This guide is written for business executives wanting to understand how to create a meaningful set of strategies for their business. Whether you have an MBA, are an MBA student, are a manager of a small or large business, or are starting a new business, this guide will teach you how to figure out a series of strategies tailored to your products or services and the markets you serve.

Ideally, it is advisable to use a third party, unbiased, moderator for all the key team meetings identified in the process; and a moderator that understands the process. I say this because an outside moderator can provide a degree of objectivity to the proceedings, which will help analyze and consolidate a strategic plan that all the interested parties can buy into without the perceived, or real, bias associated with an internal moderator. Having said that, if you are part of a small entity, this is something you can do yourself or as part of a small team, and try to remember to be open-minded to other peoples ideas and opinions.

Key Steps in the Strategic Planning Process

I have broken down the process into several bite-size steps, which will help you both gather the important input required from different individuals and will help build the much-needed consensus and understanding. The steps are as follows:

The Strategic Plan Guide

1. Gather input on the market place, your customers and your company from all interested parties (stakeholders).
2. Define your company's key strengths and weaknesses, the opportunities and threats your business faces, and the business issues and questions that need further exploration. This is better known as a SWOT (Strengths, Weaknesses, Opportunities & Threats) analysis.
3. Review and adjust inputs you receive from the stakeholders and condense the SWOT analysis to the most important issues relating to your business and your markets.
4. Define the most important strategies. This is simply done by pairing up your company's most important strengths and weaknesses with the most important market opportunities and threats. This requires thinking about how to maximize the company's strengths and how to overcome or minimize its weaknesses, and focusing your business efforts on the best opportunities, but also addressing the some of the threats to the company. This step can be difficult, but don't worry; I will walk you through it.
5. With the key strategies in place, it is now important to define the company goals and objectives, and to prepare the operational action plans.
6. Once the strategies are defined and business goals established, it is important to bring the team back together to review the strategies and to make sure nothing has been missed. Make any final corrections necessary. Then make sure goals and objectives are reflective of the strategies. Now you can prepare the operational plans (covered in other books in the *Fast-Track Business Expert Series* ™).
7. Time to put the strategy into practice and implement the plan.

The Strategic Plan Guide

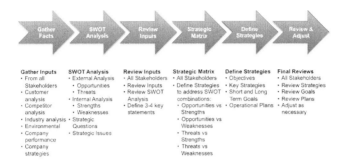

For the Entrepreneur and Start Up Company

If you are starting up or running a small company, you may not need to perform an extensive analysis and process, but I would advise you walking through the different steps and using the templates I provide at the back of the book. By answering many of the questions I provide in the detailed steps of the strategic planning process section (the next section), you will quickly be able to fill out the templates and derive several key strategies that you should employ to make your company successful.

DETAILED STEPS IN THE STRATEGIC PLANNING PROCESS

1. Gather input on strategic issues from Stakeholders

First, who are the stakeholders? In a mid size to large company, this would be your executive team (the president and vice presidents), and the top team of management (directors, functional experts), who would provide most of the input and analysis. In a smaller company, it may be just one team of senior staff, and in a start up it may be just you, or you and your co-founders. Whether small or large, I strongly suggest adding a few external experts to the mix, whether it be market experts, technical experts and, or customers. I would strongly advise against using a family member or friend who is not familiar with small businesses.

After identifying all stakeholders ask for input on the following parameters and answer as many questions as you can as fully as you can:

External strategic influences:

- Customers: Who are your customers? What are their motivations and needs? Are there different market segments you are addressing? If you are not sure, try a market survey using Twitter, Wordpress blogs or good old paper. Where are your customers located geographically?
- Competition: Who are your competition today and who are the emerging companies that you think will compete with you in the future? What are their products and how do they stack up against your product or service? What are their sales, market share growth, profits, and their strengths and weaknesses? How do they position their products? What is their pricing? How are they promoting and advertising their products?

- Industry: How would you describe your industry in terms of size, growth, structure, entry and exit barriers, distribution systems, other trends, and key success factors?
- Environment: Define the impact of technology, government regulations, the economy, cultural factors, demographics, and information needs, on your business and your products and services.

Internal strategic influences:

- Performance: How would you describe your company's performance in terms of sales, market share, return on assets (ROA)? How are your products performing? Are they profitable? Are your manufacturing costs as low as possible? How would you describe your, new product development? How would you assess your employees?
- Other Internal Factors: What have been your past, and what are your current, strategies? Did they work and give the expected results? Does your company posses any standout organization capabilities? How would you describe your company's constraints, financial resources, and flexibility to move into other markets or product types?

External strategic opportunities and threats:

When reviewing your analysis of external factors, what would you define as the greatest opportunities and threats to your business?
- Opportunities?
- Threats?

Internal strategic strengths and weaknesses:

When reviewing your analysis of the strategic internal factors, what would you define as your company's greatest strengths and weaknesses?
- Strengths?
- Weaknesses?

The Strategic Plan Guide

Strategic Questions and Issues:

Finally, after all the analysis you have completed, what are the outstanding questions and issues that need further investigation or analysis to ensure your company's success?
- Strategic questions?
- Strategic issues?

It makes sense to start with an uninhibited list of everyone's thoughts and analyses, which can then be condensed down into a shorter list. In summary, the analysis should contain answers to the questions raised above.

Situation Analysis Summary Chart

SITUATION ANALYSIS
External Analysis
• **Customer analysis**: Segments, motivations, needs, location.
• **Competitive analysis**: Products, performance, share, strengths and weaknesses, pricing, costs, profitability.
• **Industry analysis**: Markets, segments, size, growth, structure, entry barriers, distribution, trends, key success factors, profitability.
• **Environmental analysis**: Technology, government, economic, cultural, demographics, information needs
• **Opportunities?** Define any specific business opportunities for the company.
• **Threats?** Define any specific business threats the company faces.
Internal Analysis
• **Performance analysis**: Sales, profits, Return On Assets (ROA), market share, product performance, relative cost, new product activity, employee attitude.
• **Determinants of Strategic Options**: Past /current

strategy, organizational capabilities and constraints, financial resources and constraints, flexibility.
- **Strengths?** Define any specific strengths of the company. What is your value proposition? What is your competitive advantage? What is your value chain?
- **Weaknesses?** Define any specific weaknesses the company possesses.

Strategic Questions and Issues
- **Strategic Questions?** Define any specific strategic questions the company should address.
- **Strategic Issues?** Define any specific strategic issues the company should address as part of its strategic plan.

The more detail you put into this analysis, the more you will get out of it. Do not take anything for granted – check it with objective facts where possible, particularly when examining markets and market segments, customer needs and motivations and how those markets are changing. Similarly with the competitive analysis, make sure you are as objective as possible, gather as many facts as possible and solicit the competitor's customers for their opinions.

The opportunities and threats you face should derive from the external analysis, and the strengths and weaknesses are really a reflection of your company's status in light of the competition, your customer's needs and the products and services you are able to provide. Be careful with the strengths and weaknesses, there is a tendency to play up the strengths and play down the weaknesses. It is important to be as honest as possible.

It may be helpful during this process to try to define your current value proposition, and to define your sustainable competitive advantage?

Value Proposition:

One definition of a value proposition is: the unique value

your business provides to your customers. It is, in other words, the perceived value created when you meet the so-called unmet need of your target market. More simply, it is the benefit a customer receives when they buy your product or service.

Sustainable Competitive Advantage:

A sustainable competitive advantage is an attribute or group of attributes that allows a company to outperform its competitors and is not easily reproduced, thus imparting a long-term benefit.

Defining Your SWOT Analysis:

In defining the best opportunities to pursue, remember that the biggest markets are not always the best. Look at the market segments carefully, where do you have the biggest advantage, look at the profitability of each segment. You may be able to dominate a segment with good profitability, which may outweigh pursuing a larger, more competitive market with lower profitability and less chance to be successful.

Similarly, the high growth markets may also not be the best fit for your strategy. Look at the profitability and making sure you are realistic about pricing, particularly if there are a lot of competitors jumping into that segment. Can you dominate it? Can you price profitably and drive more business with better margins or is it just the growth and potential size that is attracting you? It may not be the best area for your business.

Where are you gaining market share and where are you losing it? More importantly why is this the case? Look to your competition for the answer and what they are offering? Better still ask your customers – they will tell you? This input can be vital to setting your strategy, raising strategic issues, directing your development of your next products or services, and determining if these market segments are where you want to be.

2. Define SWOT Analysis and any Strategic Questions & Issues

After all the analysis has been collected, it is time to figure out the SWOT analysis. From the various inputs you should be able to determine a long list of opportunities, threats, strengths and weaknesses.
- *External factors:* Define key opportunities and threats in the market place.
- *Internal factors:* Define key strengths and weaknesses of the company.
- Define key strategic questions and issues that still need to be understood and, or addressed.

SWOT ANALYSIS

OPPORTUNITIES	STRENGTHS
• • • • • •	• • • • • •
THREATS	**WEAKNESSES**
• • • • • •	• • • • • •
STRATEGIC QUESTIONS AND ISSUES?	
• • • • • • •	

3. Stakeholder meeting to review and adjust inputs and to define strategic matrix

- Review inputs and the SWOT analysis with all stakeholders and adjust as necessary.
- Boil down the SWOT list to 3 or 4 key statements for each component.
- Make sure this is a fair representation of the current market and the company.

CONDENSED SWOT ANALYSIS

OPPORTUNITIES	STRENGTHS
• • • •	• • • •
THREATS	**WEAKNESSES**
• • • •	• • • •
STRATEGIC QUESTIONS AND ISSUES? • • • •	

CONDENSED SWOT: Condensing the SWOT analysis is often one of the hardest tasks, but you cannot focus on everything, so you need to make some decisions as to what are the most important opportunities to pursue, what are some of the most strategic threats you face, but also what are your greatest strengths that you can exploit, and the weaknesses that require attention so that you can achieve your objectives.

4. Strategic Matrix: Define Strategic Imperatives to address SWOT and key strategic issues.

With the key stakeholders, draw up a SWOT Matrix as shown below by creating a 3 by 3 grid and marking the two far right columns "Strengths" and "Weaknesses" and the two bottom rows, "Opportunities" and "Threats". Add the bullet points from the SWOT Matrix. This now allows you to consider the combination of the different attributes you have defined in each of the SWOT categories. It is the contemplation of the two sets of attributes that challenges you to think about the important strategies your company needs to survive and prosper:

- Opportunities versus Strength: What are the strategies the company should adopt to address the major opportunities that utilizes the company's key strengths?
- Opportunities versus Weaknesses: What are the strategies the company should adopt to address the major opportunities and help overcome some of the company's key weaknesses?
- Threat versus Strength: What are the strategies the company should adopt to address the major threats the company faces by utilizing some of its key strengths?
- Threat versus Weakness: What are some of the strategies the company should adopt to address the major threats the company faces and also help the company overcome some of its key weaknesses?

See the next chart.

STRATEGIC MATRIX

STRATEGIC MATRIX	STRENGTHS • • • •	WEAKNESSES • • • •
OPPORTUNITIES • • • •	Strategies to address opportunities that utilize strengths	Strategies to address opportunities that overcome weaknesses
THREATS • • • •	Strategies to address threats that utilize strengths	Strategies to address threats that overcome weaknesses

The strategies that are developed through this process will be your strategic imperatives: each strategy should be included in various functional plans for implementation.

For Example: one of the strategies in the OPPORTUNITIES/STRENGTHS box should be your value proposition – the major unmet need of your customer being the "Opportunity" and the product or service that meets that need and provides your customers with the benefits they want, being the "Strength". Similarly, your sustainable competitive advantage is a real strength and differentiates you from the competition and will do for some time, and so should be married to an unmet need if it exists. This could certainly help over come a real threat from a competitor and so should appear in the THREATS/STRENGTHS box too.

An example of a weakness may be a lack of new products or poor development capabilities, but you may have identified some real market opportunities too? One solution might be to consider buying in or developing a product to meet that need if it makes sense in your overall strategy and if your cash flow can afford it? In

The Strategic Plan Guide

this case a product acquisition strategy or product development strategy should be added to the OPPORTUNITIES /WEAKNESSES box. Similarly, you may find that one of the reasons you are not getting certain customers business is that your competition offers a basic service that you do not. It may make sense to offer this service too, which should be added to the THREATS /WEAKNESSES box of the strategic matrix.

Remember to challenge yourself and your team to think hard about each strategy, which is suggested and to make sure that it truly addresses both sets of attributes you are discussing. You may end up with a list of strategies that is too long for you to implement all of them effectively. Don't worry; the next step will help you deal with that.

5. Define Key Strategies, set goals & objectives, prepare operational action plans

From the SWOT Matrix choose the Strategic Imperatives that will enable you to achieve your business objectives. Five or six strategic imperatives are about as much as most companies can manage with any degree of success. Choose too many and you risk the chance of over diluting your efforts and achieving little. Choose too few, and you may miss an important opportunity, or neglect a weakness, which could prove vital to your existence. So choose wisely! If there are strategies that you decide not to adopt, put them to one side for now, but don't forget to review them again at the next strategic review cycle.

Once you have your list of strategic imperatives you want to pursue it is important to convert them into a workable operational plan by ensuring they are adopted and adapted by each functional group and cross-functional team to provide an overlapping and reinforced plan that can be implemented.

I personally, like to start with goals for the year for the company from which the more detailed function-related plans can evolve. These goals should include your strategic imperatives as well as define some of the financial outcomes you expect because of your strategies.

The functional plans will vary by company and by the strategic imperatives, but for an early stage biotech company, for example, the operational plans would probably include the following:

- Research and Development Plan
- Marketing and Sales Plan (or Business Development Plan)
- Manufacturing Plan
- Financing Plan
- Human Resource Plan

The Strategic Plan Guide

- Business Plan

You can adapt this list to your own ends, based on your strategic imperatives and I will cover some of them in future books in the *Fast-Track Business Expertise Series* ™.

6. Final Stakeholder Review and Adjustment.

Arrange a final review with all stakeholders to ensure the strategy makes sense and that nothing critical was missed. I have found the best timing for this meeting to be after the strategic imperatives have been chosen, and after the companies goals for the next year have been drafted, but before any significant work has been performed on the operational and functional plans.

It really helps to send around the draft Strategic Plan several days before you meet to give everyone a chance to see what made it into the plan and what did not, but also to see the logic developed and the solutions that evolved. Now is the time to identify any weaknesses in the plan to change it before everyone agrees to a final approach. This is a vital meeting where all stakeholders should be present and the external experts too, so that various opinions can be heard and discussed. Using an expert third-party facilitator* can really help in this meeting, but again if you cannot afford the luxury, then try to be as unbiased as possible.

After the discussion, adjust the strategy as necessary, finalize it, and ensure the operational plans include each of the key strategies.

7. Implement

With the strategy, goals and operational plans in place, it is time to implement. I will cover the development of various operational plans in future books in the *Fast-Track Business Expertise Series* ™, along with implementation and execution techniques to ensure success.

---

* MP Consulting Services specializes in facilitating strategic planning and can provide support from either its USA or Europe centers.

The Strategic Plan Guide

Strategic Plan Templates

To help you prepare your own strategic plan, I have included a series of Strategic Plan Templates to guide your inputs and process:

- Strategic Plan Template 1: Strategic Inputs
- Strategic Plan Template 2: The SWOT Analysis
- Strategic Plan Template 3: The Condensed SWOT Analysis
- Strategic Plan Template 4: The Strategic Matrix
- Strategic Plan Template 5: The Strategic Imperatives

STRATEGIC PLAN TEMPLATE - 1

COMPANY NAME:_____
DATE: _____

STRATEGIC INPUTS (ALL STAKEHOLDERS)

STRATEGIC AREA	INPUT
External Analysis	
• **Customer analysis**: Segments, motivations, needs, location.	
• **Competitive analysis**: Products, performance, share, strengths and weaknesses, pricing, costs, profitability.	
• **Industry analysis**: Size, growth, structure, entry barriers, distribution, trends, key success factors, profitability.	
• **Environmental analysis**: Technology, government, economic, cultural, demographics, information needs	
• **Opportunities?** Define any specific business opportunities for the company	
• **Threats?** Define any specific business threats the company faces.	

The Strategic Plan Guide

Internal Analysis	
• **Performance analysis**: Sales, profits, Return On Assets (ROA), market share, product performance, relative cost, new product activity, employee attitude.	
• **Determinants of Strategic Options**: Past /current strategy, organizational capabilities and constraints, financial resources and constraints, flexibility.	
• **Strengths?** Define any specific strengths of the company.	
• **Weaknesses?** Define any specific weaknesses the company possesses.	
Strategic Questions and Issues	
• **Strategic Questions And Issues?** Define any specific strategic questions or issues the company should address.	

STRATEGIC PLAN TEMPLATE - 2

COMPANY NAME: _____
DATE: _____

THE SWOT ANALYSIS

OPPORTUNITIES	STRENGTHS
•	•
•	•
•	•
•	•
•	•
•	•
•	•
•	•
THREATS	**WEAKNESSES**
•	•
•	•
•	•
•	•
•	•
•	•
•	•
•	•

STRATEGIC QUESTIONS AND ISSUES?
-
-
-
-
-
-
-
-

STRATEGIC PLAN TEMPLATE – 3

COMPANY NAME:_____
DATE: _____

THE CONDENSED SWOT ANALYSIS

OPPORTUNITIES	STRENGTHS
<ul><li></li><li></li><li></li><li></li></ul>	<ul><li></li><li></li><li></li><li></li></ul>
THREATS	**WEAKNESSES**
<ul><li></li><li></li><li></li><li></li></ul>	<ul><li></li><li></li><li></li><li></li></ul>
STRATEGIC QUESTIONS AND ISSUES?	
<ul><li></li><li></li><li></li><li></li></ul>	

STRATEGIC PLAN TEMPLATE – 4

COMPANY NAME: _____
DATE: _____

THE STRATEGIC MATRIX

STRATEGIC MATRIX	STRENGTHS • • • • •	WEAKNESSES • • • • •
OPPORTUNITIES • • • • •		
THREATS • • • • •		

STRATEGIC PLAN TEMPLATE – 5

COMPANY NAME:_____
DATE: _____

THE STRATEGIC IMPERATIVES

STRATEGY #	STRATEGIC IMPERATIVE
Strategic Imperative 1	
Strategic Imperative 2	
Strategic Imperative 3	
Strategic Imperative 4	
Strategic Imperative 5	
Strategic Imperative 6	

ABOUT THE AUTHOR

MARK A. PHILIP

Mark Philip has over 20 years experience in managing businesses, both small and large, primarily in the pharmaceutical, biotechnology and medical device industry. With expertise in strategic planning, operations, product development, sales and marketing, business development, Mark has orchestrated multiple turnarounds, built product pipelines, launched new products, sold companies and created significant shareholder value.

After holding a succession of senior executive positions in biotechnology, pharmaceutical and medical device companies in Europe, the USA and Asia, Mark has also provided consulting services to a number of companies from a broad array of business sectors.

After seeing the need for professional people in many different business environments to better understand basic business principles, Mark Philip has prepared a series of course materials to help Business Executives succeed in any business setting. From his coaching of many executives in both large and small companies, Mark has created the *Fast-Track Business Expert Series ™* - a range of books and courses detailing the core skills and strategies that will help you acquire expert business experience in just a few hours.

Mark has a bachelor's degree in Applied Biology and a PhD in Stem Cell Research from Nottingham Trent University (formerly Trent Polytechnic) in the UK. After becoming The Leukemia Research Fund Postdoctoral Research Fellow at Nottingham University, Mark completed an MBA in marketing and strategy at the Lake Forest Graduate School of Management in Chicago, USA and an Advanced Leadership Course at Harvard University.

THE *FAST-TRACK BUSINESS EXPERTISE SERIES* ™ OF BOOKS AND COURSES.

After seeing the need for professional people in many different business environments to better understand basic business principles, Mark Philip has prepared a series of course materials to help Business Executives succeed in any business setting. From his coaching of many executives in both large and small companies, Mark has created the *Fast-Track Business Expert Series* ™ - a range of books and courses detailing the core skills and strategies that will help you acquire expert business experience in just a few hours.

Course Series
- The Strategic Plan Guide
- The Business Plan Guide
- The Marketing Plan Guide
- The Public Relations Plan Guide
- The Social Media Primer
- The Time Management Guide
- The Business Continuity Guide
- The Negotiations Guide
- The Effective Business Meetings Guide
- The Due Diligence Guide
- The Finding Your Ideal Job Guide

MP CONSULTING SERVICES

MP Consulting Services specializes in the areas of strategic planning, leadership, marketing and social media. Mark Philip, principal at MPCS, has over 20 years experience in managing businesses, both small and large, has orchestrated multiple turnarounds, built product pipelines, launched new products, sold companies and created significant shareholder value. Let me know how I can help you with your business challenge, or help train your organization to deal with today's competitive business challenges.

FREE GUIDES AVAILABLE FROM MP CONSULTING SERVICES

- Strategic Planning Guide.
- Business Plan Guide.
- Marketing Plan Guide.
- Public Relations Plan Guide.
- Social Media Primer.
- Time Management Guide.
- Business Continuity Guide.
- Negotiations Guide.
- Effective Business Meetings Guide.
- Due Diligence Guide.
- Blog Series.

To read more from Mark Philip, please subscribe to his blog, which can be found at: http://mpconsulting.wordpress.com

The Strategic Plan Guide

For More Information: visit my blog at
http://mpconsulting.wordpress.com
or visit my
LinkedIn account at
http://www.linkedin.com/in/markpconsulting

Made in the USA
Middletown, DE
21 November 2022